GW00493890

Contents

Foreword

It gives me great pleasure to introduce this new short history of Students' Union UCL. UCL's Student Life Strategy states: "Students' development often takes place outside formal educational settings, through the networks they build, relationships they form, and experiences they have. Student life, any alumnus will tell you, is about the friends they met, where they lived, the extra-curricular activities they were involved in, the sports they played, societies they led, music and drama groups they performed in, the volunteering projects in which they participated, and the leadership roles they held." Students' Union UCL has been at the heart of these wonderful experiences for our students for the past 130 years, making a unique contribution to the university experience for generations of UCL students.

Students' Union UCL has been a very special organisation. It was the first of its kind in the country, and remains to this day, unique in the breadth and diversity of its services for students. As we mark the Union's 130th anniversary, it is the perfect time to celebrate the organisation's many achievements since 1893 as well as to look ahead to its exciting plans for the future.

UCL has been extremely fortunate to have such a forward thinking and active students' union, which has consistently been at the forefront of social change. Right from the start, our student leaders took on ambitious projects, such as the 1897 purchase of a sports ground which cemented the Union's role leading sports at UCL, which continues to this day. In the 1940s, before the creation of the NHS, the Union developed its Health Union to ensure that all UCL students could receive free healthcare. In the 1960s and 70s, the Union was at the forefront of campaigns against apartheid in South Africa and for equal rights for the LGBT+ community in the UK. This proud tradition of progressive thinking and bold action continues with our student leaders today. As Chair of Council, I have had the pleasure of working with a group of remarkable student officers over the past few years, who have guided the Students' Union through the Covid pandemic and played a key role in renewing and developing its services for students. The Union now leads one of the largest genuinely student-led extracurricular activities programme in the world and has a growing national and international reputation for the quality of its work.

Council colleagues and I want to see Students' Union UCL continue to prosper and flourish in the decades to come. This is why we have recently agreed our new Strategy for Student Life that was co-written with the Students' Union, which plans for the largest ever expansion of extracurricular activity at our university. We are in full support of the Students' Union's efforts to explore opportunities to improve its facilities, including of the Union's long-term vision for a fit for purpose home for the Union, as well as improved facilities for sports.

UCL greatly cherishes and values the amazing history of our students' union. I hope you will enjoy reading this special publication as much as I do.

Victor Chu CBE. Chair, UCL Council.

Introduction

What is a Students' Union? Asked that question in 1948, when she applied for the position of UCL Union's Permanent Secretary, Margaret Richards – who would go on to serve in that role for 23 years – said that it was 'partly representation, partly a social focus for the students, and partly a trade union for the students: to make representation on their behalf to other people inside and outside college'.[1] This has remained the case ever since, with what is now called Students' Union UCL acting as a key part of the student experience at University College London.

The history of the organisation over the past 130 years is a rich and diverse one, reflecting UCL's fascinating and often radical story since it was founded in 1826. Student societies were formed almost immediately after UCL opened, and forerunners to the Union were established in the mid-1850s, helping to provide a greater sense of unity for students studying at the College. When the men's Union Society was founded in 1893, it brought together various aspects of student life, pioneering a model that was to be widely adopted across other universities and colleges. Many of the clubs and societies that developed and grew through the twentieth century were great successes. A Union newspaper, *Pi*, founded in 1946 and which still publishes in digital form, has given a range of budding journalists and writers an opportunity to try their hand at reporting or commenting on current affairs; a panel of newspaper journalists awarded it NUS student newspaper of the year in 1957–58.[2] Film Soc, also still flourishing today, is one of the best of its kind in the country, with an unrivalled archive of historic film footage. Sport, too, has thrived as a cornerstone of student life for many, even if the Union has had to navigate the many challenges of its central London location.

When it comes to politics and international affairs, the Union has often been a crucible of debate, discussion and free speech, hosting meetings that featured high profile politicians of the time, as well as controversial figures such as Oswald Mosely. Leading students within the Union organised and implemented a successful South African scholarship fund in the mid-1960s, which brought a succession of Black students, who could not study for a degree under Apartheid, to UCL. In the 1970s, the first ever student Gay Society in the UK became a Union club. A few years later, a radical Union President abolished his own role, meaning that the Union has had no official President for nearly 50 years. Whether on women's rights, the HIV/Aids crisis or volunteering to help people in underprivileged communities, the Union has often led on the key causes of the day. Much of this is remarkable considering that the Union has been bedevilled throughout its entire existence by facilities that have never been ideal for the work and activities its members would like to take part in. The institution has been shaped not because of but despite its lack of suitable headquarters.

Books, plaques and official notices around the UCL campus often cite the founding of the Students' Union as happening in 1893. A history was commissioned in 1993 to mark the organisation's centenary. The reality, however, is not as straightforward. On one hand, the unofficial beginnings of the organisation stretch further back in time. On the other, 1893 marked the founding of the men's Union Society only, from which women were excluded. This pamphlet marks 130 years since that occasion, but it also seeks to tell the wider story about the Union's foundation, development, growth, and some of its key moments in that process.

Outside of the Students' Union UCL building on Gordon Street, Students' Union UCL.

The Early Years of Student Life at UCL

What we now know as UCL was founded on 11 February 1826 as a non-sectarian institution. A group of radical thinkers and politicians, influenced by the writings of the philosopher Jeremy Bentham, were determined to challenge the 'old order' and the established church by creating the first university in England since those at Oxford and Cambridge.[3] As the original, self-styled 'London University', it would go on to admit non-conformists, Roman Catholics, Jewish people and – later – women, opening its doors to its first group of students in October 1828.[4] Many of these students were very young and were living at home with their families or in nearby lodgings. Part of the building was incomplete and Medics dominated cohorts in the first decades. Consequently, a Medical Society was formed almost immediately. In the same year, a Debating Society was set up (although it was originally named the Literary and Philosophical Society).[5] There was even some kind of student press in this early period. Activities like societies and student-produced publications would later be considered as key elements of Union life and it is significant that such things existed from the earliest years. Even though early examples of newspapers like the *London University Chronicle*, published in 1830, only lasted for a few editions, students were not shy in criticising the authorities. There has long been a rebellious and independently minded streak amongst UCL students.[6]

Student societies flourished between the 1830s and 1893. A Reading Room Society was formed in 1858 with the primary aim of encouraging a greater sense of community amongst students.[7] Even though UCL had been secular in nature since its foundation, a Christian Association was formed in 1859 to allow those students who wanted to take part in a daily prayer meeting at lunch time to do so.[8] UCL began experimenting with admitting female students via the London Ladies' Educational Association in the late 1860s, and women were able to take degrees from 1878.[9] At this stage, men and women had separate spaces on campus and started their own societies, too, such as the Women's Debating Society, formed in 1879. In 1884, the University College Society, very much a forerunner of the Union, was founded. Its aim was to maintain friendly relationships between the College, academic staff and students. At the same time, the University College *Gazette* became the first systematic student publication.[10]

UNIVERSITY COLLEGE, LONDON.

The Members of the 𝔇𝔢𝔟𝔞𝔱𝔦𝔫𝔤 𝔖𝔬𝔠𝔦𝔢𝔱𝔶 *request the honour of the Company of* *Mr MaurceBy Eurretjeu* *and Friends, at the Annual Debate, to be held in the College,*

On Wednesday, April 18th, 1866, at 7.30 p.m.

SUBJECT:—" Is the character of Napoleon III. worthy of admiration?"
HENRY M. BOMPAS, M.A., LL.B., will open in the affirmative;
NICHOLAS J. HANNEN, B.A., will reply.

The presence of Ladies is requested.

EDWARD HENRY BUSK, M.A.,

Tea and Coffee at 7 p.m.]   *President.*

Debating Society invitation, 1866. UCL Special Collections.

Undoubtedly, a key moment in UCL's history was the formation of the men's Union Society in 1893, as a co-ordinating body for athletic clubs and wider social activity. A desire for better sporting facilities and a more suitable athletics ground were a major driving factor behind this.[11] A ground at Acton in west London was purchased in 1897 with a fund for student activities bequeathed by Henry Crabb Robinson, one of UCL's founders.[12] The Union Society came into being through a combined effort of students and staff, who formed committees and worked together to achieve a shared goal.[13] In the earliest years of the men's Union, and in that same spirit of co-operation, academic staff filled most leadership and management roles. The first President of the Union in 1893–4 was Professor Edward Schafer, a renowned professor of physiology, who in 1894 discovered the existence of adrenaline. Gregory Foster, who would later become the Provost of UCL, also acted in that role.[14]

The Union Society's stated aim was 'the promotion of social intercourse and of the means of recreation, physical and mental, of the students of the University College, and the financial success of students' clubs'. In that first year, there were 133 members, representing a small but significant proportion of the student body at the time. The men's Union represented what most students' unions across the country would eventually become, but it was the first in England to bring these elements of student life together formally under one umbrella, making it genuinely pioneering.[15] Women, however, were not included. Several years later in 1897, a separate Women's Union Society (WUS) was formed. This was done under the guidance of Rosa Morison, the Lady Superintendent of Women Students 1883–1912 and a pivotal figure in the suffrage movement at UCL.[16] She served as President of the Women's Union Society for eleven years.[17]

Rosa Morison, Lady Superintendent of Women Students, 1883–1912. UCL Special Collections.

Slade School photographed in 1905. UCL Special Collections.

The Union Society's Games Room in the late nineteenth century. UCL Special Collections.

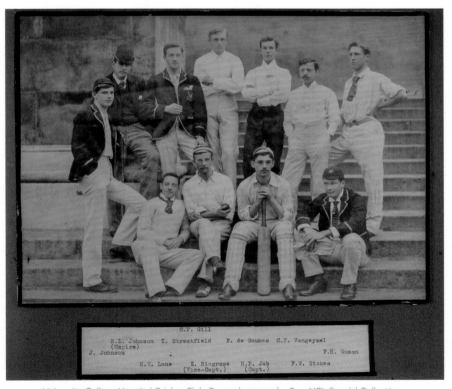

G.F. Gill

R.L. Johnson   T. Streatfield   F. de Gaumes   C.T. Vangeyzel
(Umpire)
J. Johnson   F.H. Gaman

H.W. Lane   E. Ringrose   H.P. Job   F.W. Stokes
(Vice-Capt.)   (Capt.)

University College Hospital Cricket Club, Team photograph, 1894. UCL Special Collections.

Student Culture Before the First World War

Towards the end of the nineteenth century, a stronger student culture became more evident at UCL. In 1897, the Union Society was given three rooms for its use, which opened at 9am and closed at 8.30pm every weekday.[18] The Union has always been run by a combination of a student leadership team and staff members. In 1904, a student, John Farncombe, became Union Society President for the first time, heralding a new kind of student-led culture. A couple of years later, this developed further when student officers were elected to what are now called sabbatical officer roles for the first time. This was the beginning of making the system more democratic.[19] However, in that same year, 1906, the Union splintered a little when University College Hospital Medical School detached from UCL, and a separate Medical Union was formed.[20] The distinction between the Students' Union and the Medical Union would continue to be the subject of on-and-off discussion, debate and some uncertainty for the next 100 years.

In the first decade of the twentieth century a wider range of clubs and societies was established, and the Union ensured that a core number of these would be designated as 'associate' clubs, which students did not have to pay anything to join. These centrally-funded societies were, initially, Music, Debate and Drama (later, Film Soc would be added to that list along with, intriguingly, the Jazz Society).[21] A landmark moment for these associate societies was the staging of the first student play, in 1906: Oscar Wilde's *The Importance of Being Earnest*.[22] The early twentieth century also witnessed the foundation of a Critical Society, for 'the consideration of philosophical, social, and religious questions without any restrictions as to standpoint'.[23]

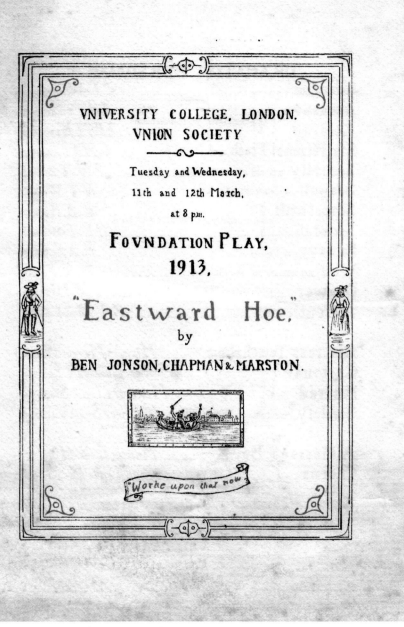

The programme for the 1913 Foundation Play, *Eastward Hoe*. UCL Special Collections.

Before the First World War physical recreation became increasingly central to some students' lives. Early sporting success was limited, not least because College teams had a relatively small number of students to choose from and many were simply too busy with their studies to get stuck in. One student, H. J. Harris, led a campaign that resulted in the roping off of Wednesday afternoons for sport from the early 1900s, which made a difference.[24] This increased activity meant that the sports ground at Acton soon became inadequate for all student sport events – it had never really been adequate, in truth – and in 1905 a site further west at Perivale was purchased by the Union, opening two years later. This was financed by much fundraising activity which also generated funds for a pavilion. This included a dedicated space for the Women's Union Society, although the men and women used separate pitches and facilities.[25] The original facilities included eighteen grass courts, two cricket squares, a grass running track, a jumping area, two football pitches, two rugby pitches and two hockey pitches.

Front cover of the UCL Union Magazine, 1904. UCL Special Collections.

This period witnessed another key development in the emergence of a certain kind of student culture at the College. In 1900, during a parade to celebrate the relief of Ladysmith in the Second Boer War, a large wooden statue which advertised tobacco was stolen by UCL students from outside a department store on nearby Tottenham Court Road. The figure, which depicted a large Scottish highlander and was one of many that stood guard outside shops in this period, became known as 'Phineas'. He became UCL's unofficial mascot, regularly being stolen from the shop and then returned as part of student pranks and rag week stunts. Students from UCL's rival college, King's, would kidnap Phineas and in turn students from UCL would capture King's mascot, Reggie the Lion. Eventually, in 1932, the department store Catesby's gave Phineas to UCL students, and he became the College's official mascot. For many more decades, Phineas was taken to sporting matches and appeared regularly on key occasion, even meeting the King and Queen in 1927. The original capture of Phineas was part of a wider rag celebration, which was an important social moment in the life of many students in this period. Rags involved light-hearted stunts, hijinks and races. There was usually a competitive element with other universities – which, in UCL's case, continued to be its great rival King's. Rag often coincided with 5th November, so bonfires were lit – in the UCL Quad until the 1950s! The concept of rag as a charity fundraising event was challenged by students in the 1960s who wanted a more meaningful engagement with local communities while the nature of rag has been re-evaluated more recently in light of its darker, sexist undertones.[26]

Inter-war shot of Phineas surrounded by students. UCL Special Collections.

The First World War and its Aftermath

The outbreak of the First World War in 1914 had a huge impact on student life and Union affairs at UCL. Studies were seriously disrupted. The numbers of male students on the roll declined sharply, buildings were requisitioned, and research was realigned to support the war effort.[27] During those war years, the Union published a 'pro patria' section in its annual handbook, listing all 'past and present members of the College known to be serving the country in some active capacity'.[28] In particular, women students had a new role to play, with some forming a Voluntary Aid Detachment (VAD). Members served in the VAD's St. Pancras-based Ambulance Squad, and some nursed in military hospitals in France. Women were finally allowed to study medicine at UCL from 1917. In the immediate aftermath of the war, students made it clear their desire 'to raise a permanent and visible Memorial to those who have fallen', with over 2,600 former or current members having undertaken service and 301 having 'laid down their lives'.[29] The goal amongst students was to erect a monument to the fallen in the form of a Great Hall, opened in 1927 in a converted church on the site on Gordon Street where the Student Centre now stands.[30]

UNIVERSITY COLLEGE
AND HOSPITAL
SOCIALIST
SOCIETY

University College and Hospital Socialist Society poster, 1930s. UCL Special Collections.

UCL's new Great Hall was opened in 1927. It was competely destroyed in the Second World War. UCL Special Collections.

The immediate post-war period witnessed other significant changes, not least because the numbers of students either entering or returning to the College rose dramatically, including large numbers of ex-servicemen on government grants.[31] Discussions between the Men's and Women's unions had continued over the years on matters such as the sports ground and refectory dances, but no regular joint committee of men and women was formed until 1919.[32] This was called the Inter Union Standing Committee and came into being to the apparent 'delight of the student body as a whole'.[33] Under the auspices of the committee, a new range of societies was established or re-formed, some of them reflecting the fashions and concerns of the 1920s. A Toc H Club acted 'as a living memorial to those who died in the Great War'. It drew its members from 'academic staff, students and servants' to continue 'the spirit of fellowship ... which existed among the troops'.[34] A German Society was formed in in 1920 in order to try and make the study of Germany more accessible. By the early 1930s there was an International Society, reflecting the fact that around a quarter of the student body came from outside the UK by the inter-war period.[35] The College's Choral Society became the Glee Club, to make it feel less formal.[36] Specific clubs for women included badminton, boating, cricket, gymnastics, hockey, lacrosse, lawn tennis, netball, swimming, a common room tea club, and a debating society.[37] Large numbers of students also moved to the left politically and there was an active Socialist Society and support for relief efforts during the Spanish Civil War.

This higher number of students and the greater levels of collaboration between the Unions required more space and resources, and the Union was allocated a specific room in the Great Hall for society members to work in. This was symbolically important, as it placed students and the Union at the heart of the College, although it demonstrated that space in this central London location was a problem that would only become more acute.[38] In the inter-war period, 'few social events are complete without a sing-song' and the Union began publishing a Student's Song Book in 1926 that included a new song by the poet John Drinkwater composed to mark UCL's centenary.[39] The inter-war years also saw the emergence of a stronger student press. In 1937, a new Union newspaper, *Phineas* (named after the by now-official mascot), was launched. This was largely applauded for dealing with UCL topics like lack of resources and long queues for the refectory. Indeed, the standard of catering at the College was a regular gripe. *Phineas* allowed students to write opinion pieces on a variety of matters that covered serious and less formal issues.[40] Much of this was of course disrupted again on the outbreak of war in 1939.

Women's Union Society
University College. London 1931.

The Women's Union Society, 1931. UCL Special Collections.

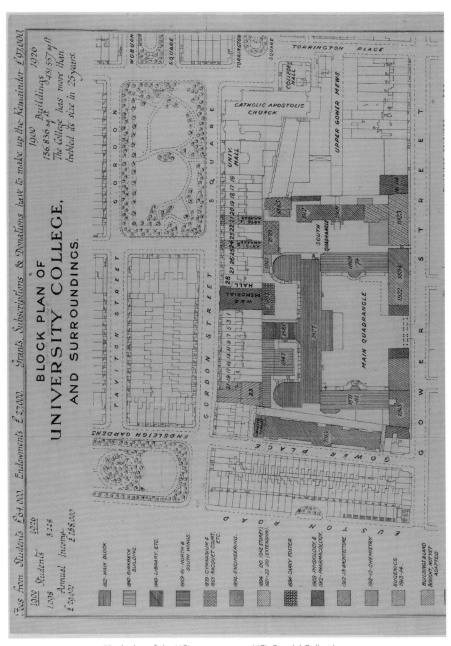

Block plan of the UCL campus, 1923. UCL Special Collections.

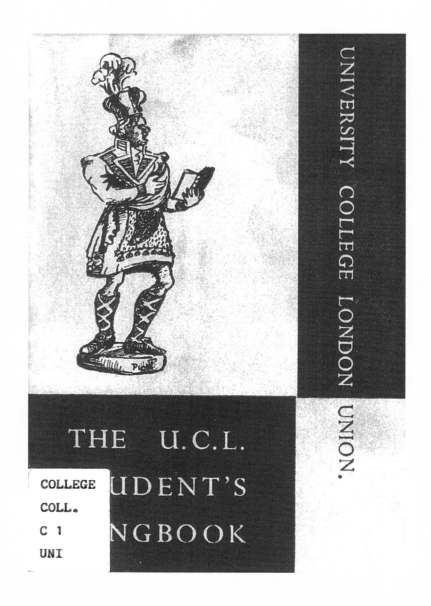

The UCL Student's Songbook. UCL Special Collections.

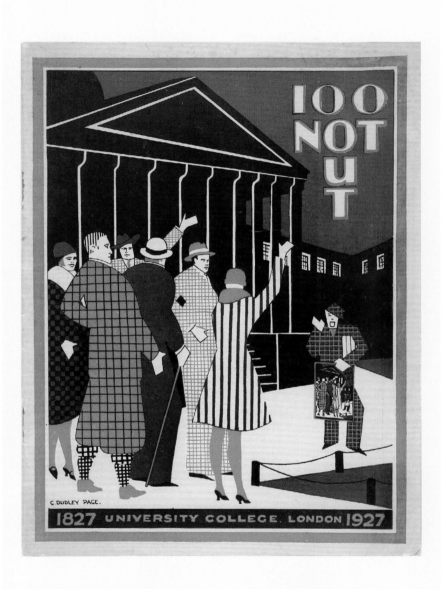

Cover of the rag mag published to mark UCL's centenary in 1927. UCL Special Collections.

Evacuation and Bomb Damage: UCL in the 1940s

The Second World War posed an even greater challenge for the Union than the First World War had. Fears of bombing raids meant that students were evacuated out of London. Numbers on the roll, particularly men, again dropped sharply. Slade students went to Oxford, architects to Cambridge, engineers to Swansea, scientists to Bangor, and arts, economics and chemistry students to Aberystwyth. Medics were split between Cardiff, Bangor and Sheffield.[41] Even Phineas was evacuated out of London, although he was at one point kidnapped by students at Swansea. As that kidnapping demonstrated, some attempts were made to maintain a Union-focused student culture, but nothing substantial was possible when members were dispersed all over the country. A student publication, *New Phineas*, an amalgamation of *Phineas* and a second publication, the *University College Magazine*, was created as a means of trying to keep the links between these scattered students alive.[42] The Union handbook talked forlornly of trying to 're-mind all students of the traditions of University College London, which evacuation has made difficult to maintain'.[43] Ultimately, however, because of the long duration of the war, many UCL students never took any classes in London. For Diana Armfield, a Slade Student from this period who was interviewed about her student life in 2022, studying with UCL consisted of living above a sweet shop in Oxford.[44] The hardships not just of war but of being evacuated did result in the Union setting up its first dedicated Hardship Fund, named the Committee for the Alleviation of Student Hardship (C.A.S.H).[45]

Meanwhile, in London, a great moment of tragedy struck the College. The Great Hall, itself a poignant legacy of the First World War, was destroyed in the Blitz of 1940. Much of the UCL site was also damaged, in some cases very seriously, and this had a direct impact on student life. The space allocated to the Union shrank because of the need to rationalise what undamaged space there was left.[46] Students, returning to a bomb-ravaged site, were told by the Union handbook that UCL 'as it stands to-day is but a shell of its former glory'.[47] One Chemistry student, Alwyn Davies, who was starting his studies in the immediate aftermath of the conflict, remembered how his department was 'in a dreadful condition and the first thing that all the research students did was to clear it up'.[48]

Second World War bomb damage at UCL, including the destruction of the Great Hall and parts of the main building's cloisters. UCL Special Collections.

Drama Society photographed in 1948. Students' Union UCL.

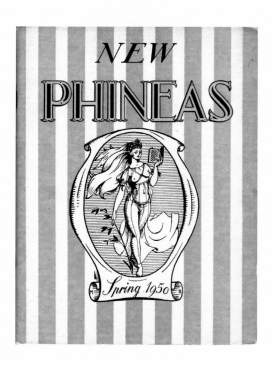

The Spring 1950 front cover of *New Phineas*. UCL Special Collections.

Reconstructing Student Life

Despite the damage of war, and the almost-total dismantling of everyday student life, the immediate post-war years are amongst the most significant in the Union's history. The pace of change was dramatic and it is striking to note how much happened in such a short space of time when the College faced so many challenges. Perhaps most significant is that a joint Union comprising of both men and women was formed in 1946. This laid the groundwork for the future, not least because shortly afterwards, in 1948, Margaret Richards was appointed as its Permanent Secretary. She is one of the most important people in the Union's history and was reportedly 'loved by everyone at UCL', working very long hours and executing her duties efficiently until her retirement in 1971.[49] Her guidance helped shape the organisation and set a course for its future direction. Sport at UCL also entered a new phase, with facilities north of the city at Shenley coming into use in 1946. The land had been purchased by the Union in 1939 as a replacement for the ground at Perivale. However, before work could begin at the site, war broke out and the fields were used as grazing land for sheep.

When they came into operation, the facilities there were much improved. It had double the number of rugby and soccer pitches, and much better bathroom, changing and bar facilities.[50] An alternative society set up at this time was Film Soc, which would quickly develop into one of the best and most popular societies of its kind in the country, producing and screening many of its members' own films and contemporary documentaries.[51] (The film director, Christopher Nolan, cut his teeth at Film Soc in the early 1990s and later returned to film some famous scenes for his movies on the UCL site). In those immediate post-war years, and in the spirit of the politics of the time, the College established a pioneering Student Health Association to provide free healthcare for students at the point of need, before the creation of the NHS. The Union also established a Welfare Committee to help students 'on questions relating to grants, housing ... and personal difficulty'.[52]

The bar at the Shenley sportsground.. Students' Union UCL.

In the spirit of renewal in the years after the war, a new newspaper was founded in 1946 with the aim of giving students back their voice to comment on a range of College activity during a period of bleak post-war austerity. It was called *Pi*, named after the Provost, Sir David Pye – an act of deference that was of its time and would be unlikely to happen now! From the beginning, some students engaged with the paper, writing letters to it, to offer witty comment on College life, or to maintain the old tradition of complaining about inadequate facilities – of which there were many, particularly the Refectory.[53] As with all student publications, *Pi* was written and produced by a relatively small number of students, but it has nonetheless been operating in various forms ever since, making it one of the country's longer-standing student newspapers. In the post-war years, the paper presented itself as a non-political organ that would refrain from acting as a soap box. However, students had a range of political societies they could join if they wished to, from the Conservative Society through to the Revolutionary Socialist Society.[54] In Union politics, the first (and only) woman to be elected President, Sheila Fitzgerald, took up her role in 1952. She and other Union officials in these years faced 'inadequate' buildings, and financial woes. From the early 1950s, the Union was given 9 per cent of College fee income, but this did little more than provide funds for general maintenance of the amenities already in use.[55]

Despite justified complaints about facilities, these immediate post-war years included a decision to open the first Union Bar, staffed by a full-time barman called Charlie, whose wit and stories were apparently a constant source of amusement, 'even to water drinkers'.[56] The bar, opened in 1947, was situated in the South Junction and sold beer and cigarettes, but not spirits.[57] The bar was quickly judged to be the 'most popular aspect of Union activities' and 'the real common denominator of student life'.[58]

At around the same time, the Union was given a set of rooms in the nearby South Wing basement, which allowed all its offices to be located in one place (and which happened to be near the bar).[59] Prefabricated huts in the South Quadrangle housed things like table tennis tables and Debating Society events.[60] Debates were popular and topics ranged from the historical, like the reign of King John, to more philosophical, and perhaps tongue-in-cheek discussions, like 'This House [believes] life is not worth living'.[61] The Dramatic Society in this period staged many productions that were 'outside the scope of the commercial theatre'. In other words, plays or operas that were not commonly performed and which few had even heard of, like John Webster's 'The White Devil' or Bizet's 'Don Procopio' were staged at UCL, resulting in positive write ups from the national and not just the student press. For decades, such performances were close collaborations between the drama and music societies.[62]

A view of the UCL site from Gordon Street, including many of the post-war huts, that were home to many Students' Union activities. The Student Centre now sits on this site. UCL Special Collections.

Students and Social Change in the 1960s and 1970s

Despite these formative post-war years, a level of dissatisfaction with parts of student life persisted. A common grumble remained the poor standard of catering on site. One student-produced cartoon from 1956 shows catering staff in the College's cafeteria goggling in amazement at something. The caption reads: 'Gosh, he ate it!'. The Provost, Sir Ifor Evans, was filmed in this period telling a student meeting, in the context of the catering, that 'if you're not satisfied with us, go elsewhere!'[63] Problems with office space for Union officials continued, with plans eventually drawn up to move the organisation, on a temporary basis, into the old Tropical Diseases Hospital, formerly the Endsleigh Palace Hotel at 25 Gordon Street.[64] The move, which eventually took place in 1959, was neither smooth nor uncontroversial. Even in 1955, the new premises (at a time when there were 3,000 students on the roll) was described as somewhere that could not 'meet all requirements' for the Union.[65] On the eve of the Union moving into the building, it was described by the Provost as 'very far from adequate for the size of the College'.[66] Foreshadowing debates about the building that would continue up to today, students and sabbatical officers in the mid-1950s argued that the site did not occupy a central enough position in the College, and was too small for both the social and society aspects of Union life. The Union did at least maintain 'The Garage', a hut on the bombsite where the Great Hall had been. This continued to host social events, including the Saturday night 'hop' (dance) which, in the words of one female student from the early 1960s, was 'where you went to find a boyfriend'.[67] The Saturday UC disco continued to be rated highly by students at neighbouring colleges into the 1970s.[68]

Meanwhile, debate at the top of the Union over what the organisation's remit should be, and how much it should engage with 'external' matters, became much louder in the 1950s and into the 1960s. 1,200 students signed a petition in 1956 about the Soviet invasion of Hungary and students organised a silent march through the streets of London in protest at this.[69] New African-Caribbean, Pakistan and Polish societies that were set up in the '50s reflected the changing international profile of the student body and an organisation that was keen to 'look outwards' to a greater extent.[70] Indeed, one fifth of the student population by the late 1950s had come from 77 different overseas countries.[71]

The Garage, converted from a post-war hut and used for rehearsals, sports and functions. Students' Union UCL.

Walter ('Walley') Greaves, President in 1961–62, was of the view that specific UCL and student-focused issues were of most importance. He was challenged by a more radical figure, Roger Lyons, who would go on to become a trade union leader and President of the Trades Union Congress, and who was interested in taking stances on topics like nuclear weapons. Lyons felt that the Union should relate 'to the outside world' and reflected the growing student interest in left-wing causes that would intensify as the decade unfolded.[72] *Pi* mirrored this shift, focusing its coverage more on the outside world as opposed to College or Union affairs.[73] Jonathan Dimbleby, who later became a well-known journalist and broadcaster, was especially important in changing the nature of the paper during his period as editor in the late 1960s, when he created a 'Features' section and covered a much wider array of stories.[74] It was from this time that the Union began nominating key international figures as honorary President for a year. Some people, like Martin Luther King Junior or Nelson Mandela, stood the test of time. Others, such as Robert Mugabe, fair less well in hindsight![75] Although the structure of the Union still looked rather traditional in the 1960s, with a Sabbatical Officer acting each year as the 'Woman Vice President', that role was not solely for so-called 'women's issues'. As one holder of the post in the mid-1960s, Toni Griffiths, remembers:

> *I found myself ... running things, writing things, making speeches. Making speeches at dinners. Giving toasts. Holding receptions for the glorious Presidents of other university student unions and so on. And running and organising my own Ball, which was then called the Women's at Home ... All sorts of things.*[76]

Toni Griffiths as the Students' Union Woman Vice President. UCL Special Collections.

Although interest in topics including nuclear disarmament or the Vietnam War led to large-scale protests (the Labour party leader Hugh Gaitskell was booed at one meeting in 1962 where he expressed his support for the UK's nuclear deterrent[77]), the issue of Apartheid South Africa stirred the greatest passions amongst UCL students.[78] Lyons and his successor as Union President, Tom McNally, oversaw the introduction of a scholarship scheme that would bring a Black South African student to UCL.[79] This campaign, and subsequent ones, were launched with a rally in the Quad, and much fanfare.[80] Lyons and his team carefully and cleverly portrayed themselves as 'only concerned with this policy as it affects universities in South Africa ... the admission or exclusion of a student on the basis of the colour of his skin is quite contrary to everything that University College London represent'.[81] By having a well-focused campaign, they were able to achieve clear results and a series of Black scholars from South Africa came to UCL over the course of subsequent years.

By the late 1960s, an enormous social and cultural shift in parts of British life was underway and this was particularly noticeable in the student population. The satire boom, for example, was marked at UCL by the formation of Jaundice, a satirical society that staged skits to skewer old-fashioned, stuffy views.[82] Within the space of ten years, undergraduates had turned from relatively formal and deferential figures into students who appeared outwardly 'youthful' in a way that we would recognise today.

Whereas they had once named the newspaper after the Provost, the arrival of a new one – Lord Annan – in 1966, warranted a profile where the new head of College was described, first and foremost, as 'bald headed'.[83] This was aided by the lowering of the age of majority (i.e. legal adulthood) at the very end of 1969, meaning that university authorities no longer acted as the legal guardians of their students.

S. AFRICAN SCHOLAR ARRIVES AT LONG LAST

McNally Greets Lyttleton at Airport

ON THURSDAY last, just before 4 p.m., 26-year-old Lyttleton Mngquikana landed at London Airport. The South African Scholar's first comment to President Tom McNally once they had cleared the Immigration Office —"When do lectures start?"—is surely an encouraging sign.

Lyttleton left East London, South Africa, yesterday afternoon our time and changed planes without a hitch at Johannesburg. On arrival at London Airport he was met by McNally, Gerry Johnson, Chairman of JACARI, and two female cousins, who as far as he could remember he had not met before.

Although the journey itself was uneventful, the preparations prior to his leaving South Africa were most disturbing.

"I had almost given up hope of getting over here," he said.

As Lyttleton had left South Africa on an Exit Permit, and the Home Office had stipulated that anyone entering the country without a passport did so at the discretion of the Immigration Officer, McNally went to the airport armed with the necessary documents to ensure Mngquikana's speedy admittance. In fact once the plane had landed, albeit 25 minutes late, the entire Customs and Immigration routine was completed in under 15 minutes.

On leaving London Airport Mngquikana was taken by College minibus to Ramsay Hall, where he is to live for the rest of the year. From there the Presidential Party wound its inevitable way to bar, where McNally was heard to mutter

TRIAL AND ERROR

IN APRIL 1964 the South African Scholarship Fund was set up to enable a non-white South African, deprived of educational opportunities in his country by the racial laws, to pursue a full-time degree course at University College. Within eight weeks the target of £2,000 had been reached.

However, Livingstone Mrwetyana, the student selected to take up the scholarship in October '64 was detained by the South African authorities, and later imprisoned for four years. £250 was raised to finance his appeal, the result of which is not known.

The award was held open for Mrwetyana until March of this year, when a general meeting decided that further applications should be invited. Lyttleton Mngquikana was accepted in April.

The strenuous efforts undertaken on behalf of the Union to ensure that Lyttleton would satisfy Home Office conditions for Immigration led to a series of bewildering, frustrating and near-disastrous encounters with officialdom. At the

LATE PI BUT NOT STALE

This delay enabled us to cover fully the South

RUGGER 'N' JAZZ

PART of Tom McNally's job at the airport was to give Lyttleton his first £100 cheque. An attempt by PI to photograph this satisfying event was unfortunately foiled by the President's exuberance. Commented Mngquikana: "Tom should be good company to begin with." Although, as Lyttleton assured us, he has come to UC mainly to work, he is a keen

Students' Union President Tom McNally greets the first South African scholar, Lyttleton Mngquikana in October 1965. UCL Special Collections.

1960s Students' Handbooks. UCL Special Collections.

UK universities did not experience turbulent student protests to the same extent as places like Paris in 1968, but politics and protest certainly become more of a feature of some students' lives. At UCL, like many other universities and colleges, this manifested itself most clearly in students lobbying for a much greater say in how the institution was run. Luckily, Lord Annan was relatively sympathetic to this, and the beginnings of student representation on governance committees began in 1969. A greater liaison between the College authorities and elected sabbatical officers therefore has its genesis in this period. However, accommodation continued to be a bone of contention amongst undergraduates. The central London location made things like halls of residence trickier to provide. University Hall in Ealing had offered rooms for men before the war and growing demand led to UCL converting some town houses for accommodation. The opening of the purpose-built Ramsey Hall in 1964, however, marked a major moment for UCL students. Goldsmid House opened in the prime location of Oxford Street in 1968 at the same time as a self-catering hall, Ifor Evans, in Camden.[84]

Shake-ups at the Union

In a more localised sense, cultural change was also taking place at the Union. Michael Freeman replaced Margaret Richards as the Union's Permanent Secretary in 1971, although the role was technically split in two, with Margo Levine taking the post of Commercial Manager and dealing with shops and catering – a reflection of the importance of these elements of Union life.[85] Freeman faced a range of challenges when he took up the role, most of which related to lack of space. The Central Collegiate Building (later renamed the Bloomsbury Theatre) had been opened in 1969, funded in part by a £100,000 benefaction from Lord Marks of Marks and Spencer's fame.[86]

Central Collegiate Building when it opened, now the Bloomsbury Theatre. UCL Special Collections.

It provided extra rooms and many more sports facilities for students, as well as housing the offices for a range of clubs and societies. To the frustration of students, however, it failed to deliver on the long standing promise of a proper new building for the Students' Union. But the numbers coming to study at UCL continued to rise and the Bloomsbury site offered little in the way of flexibility. In 1979, a large gym was built in the Central Collegiate Building, which proved popular.[87] However, it spoke to the issues the Union continued to face that the gym was built around the theatre.[88] Noise from the former could be heard in the latter, which was far from ideal given that many students wished to use these facilities at the same time.[89] Throughout the 1970s and 1980s, plans to expand the Union, or move to a new building, were carefully drawn up on the site of the original Great Hall on Gordon Street, where the Student Centre now stands, the case was made, but all such schemes ended in disappointment.[90]

The wider social and cultural change of the 1960s was starting to impact many aspects of the Union by the early 1970s. Women students were involved in the first women's liberation marches of the early 1970s. In 1972, a Mathematics Ph.D. student from Australia, Jamie Gardiner, took the bold move of setting up a GaySoc, to represent gay students and campaign for their rights (the partial decriminalisation of homosexual acts between men in private had only taken place in 1967). Remembering giong to the Union to try and set up the club, Jamie recalls how:

> *Joan was there and I looked in through the little window, like a ticket box sort of window and I said hello, I'm wondering how you set up a club, a society. 'Oh' she said, 'you fill in this form' and so we chatted a little bit about the form and she said 'what's the name' or 'what's the society for?', and I said 'gay students', I don't remember precisely what I said but anyway I definitely said it's a gay society, or words to that effect. 'Oh' she said, 'OK'. And we continued chatting about filling in the form and having felt heart in mouth at actually saying the word 'gay' out like that, it was: good, well this is OK, this is easy. And so I filled in the form and all of the Student Union societies were something Soc, so we were GaySoc...[91]*

Members of UCL's Gay Soc, including Jamie Gardner, at the NUS Conference, Exeter in 1973.

Initially, GaySoc took an actively political stance, presenting itself as both a social outlet for what it guessed were the '400 or so homosexual men and women at this College' as well as a campaigning group in alliance with organisations like the Gay Liberation Front and the Campaign for Homosexual Equality, which were attempting to change the law to bring the treatment of gay people more into line with heterosexual people, particularly regarding the unequal age of consent.[92] The Union began organising a GaySoc disco on Tuesday nights, which attracted students not just from UCL but from across London.[93] Perhaps unsurprisingly, those who went to these events sometimes received abuse, that could spill over into physical violence, but Gardiner and his allies at UCL were responsible for establishing the first society of this kind in the UK. GaySoc was also responsible for encouraging the NUS to take up gay rights as a more specific issue, and to run special conferences on the matter.[94] It worked closely with the Union officers and for many years had a prominent place in the fresher's handbook (in some years, it was *the* prominent society), advertising the Society, and suggesting the best gay or gay-friendly pubs to drink in.[95]

This period also saw the beginnings of the Union discussing the environment in the kinds of language that would morph into wider concerns over the green agenda in later decades. In 1973, the Eco Action group asked: 'Are you interested in ... the problems of over-population, pollution, growth-mania, overpackaging, destruction of urban communities ... and the wastage ... encouraged by our throwaway society?'[96]

Union Administrator Michael Freeman shows Princess Anne plans for a new Union building, 1981.
Students' Union UCL.

The spirit of the times led to a general critique of hierarchy. At the Union, this resulted in one of the 'biggest shake ups in its history'. Chris Ray, the President, completely reorganised the committee structure which led to three Sabbatical officer roles of equal status. In short, Ray abolished the role of Union President at UCL, with the decision coming into effect in 1975.[97] The reaction to this radical move was mixed. Many have subsequently taken the view that one officer defaults to the President role anyway, whilst others have remarked on the egalitarian nature of the revised structure being in keeping with the spirit of the Union. More broadly, from the 1970s, there was a big expansion of student welfare provision at the Union. This developed in parallel with new discussions about issues like women's rights and concerns over sexual violence on campus, which led to a high-profile campaign and occupation in 1979.[98] Official Union publications gave hard-up students advice on squatting, telling them that 'In general, you should not worry too much about your legal position. If you act collectively with others, you will usually be fairly secure'.[99]

The gap on Gordon Street where a new Union building was proposed.
It is now filled by the Student Centre. Students' Union UCL

Into the 1980s

Through the 1980s and 1990s, demand for Union services soared as student numbers rose. Between 1986 and 1999, 12 previously separate institutions merged with UCL, including the Middlesex Hospital Medical School, the Royal Free Hospital Medical School and the School of Eastern European and Slavonic Studies.[100] By the very beginning of the '80s, the Union employed over 50 staff to ensure the smooth running of the sports facilities, theatre, cafés, bars and its various offices.[101] The bars at 25 Gordon Street were refurbished and expanded to try and accommodate the high level of demand. Evenings were often very busy, with the (in)famous cocktails night being launched in 1981.[102] This quickly became not just extremely popular with those at UCL, but with students across London. Queues to get into 25 Gordon Street would stretch around the block, partly a sign of the event's notoriety, but also a reflection of the fact that the relatively small building could only house a certain number of people due to fire regulation. In the early-1980s, the capacity of 25 Gordon Street amounted to just 6.5 per cent of the total UCL student body.[103] There was some backlash, and concern was voiced that students were drinking too much cheap alcohol at this cocktails night.[104] The visible strain that this was putting on resources intensified, with a large student occupation taking place in 1987 to demand a better Union building and more space. The opening of the Windeyer Café-Bar in 1991 helped meet some of the desperate need for more room, and it usefully operated as both a catering facility and an entertainments venue.[105] Although the Union later lost use of this space when the building was demolished. Many students also utilised the facilities at the University of London's Union (ULU), with its building on Malet Place. Facilities here were considered good, especially the cafés, bar and the swimming pool, which generations of students gratefully utilised. Actor Ricky Gervais, one of UCL's better-known former students, spent much of his time whilst a student working and socialising at ULU.[106]

Unsurprisingly, the expansion of student numbers to around 9,000 by the end of the 1980s led to an increase in the number and range of societies that the Union offered.[107] Sport remained popular and to accommodate for increased demand, fields north of Shenley were converted into extra grounds.[108] New martial arts clubs opened for students, including aikido, judo, tae kwon do, kung fu and wing chun, with judo offering specific self-defence classes to women students. The position of women in the Union and on campus more generally became the topic of discussion, with a specific Women's Officer being created in 1986.[109]

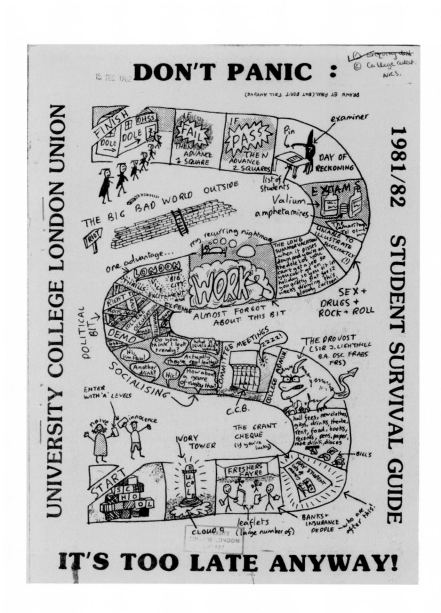

Student handbook 1981–2. UCL Special Collections.

A fourth Sabbatical officer had been added in 1983, who was responsible for Publicity and Communications, and the precise duties of the 'sabbs' changed for the next couple of decades. Significantly, with the amalgamation of the University College and Middlesex School of Medicine in 1987, a dedicated post for medical students was created.

The Union's approach to the unfolding HIV/Aids epidemic is a striking aspect of this period. Located in the midst of the capital city where infection rates were highest, the annual fresher's handbooks – and separate safe sex guides – addressed the issue head on by providing straightforward, often graphic, but undoubtedly useful advice about what did and did not constitute safe sex.[110] The Union even made the decision to give people advice on how to inject drugs, if they were doing so, safely so as to lessen the risk of contracting HIV, including tips on 'sterilising your works'.[111] The wider politics of the era, including the discrimination faced by gay men in particular because of the Aids crisis, led to the Union formulating its first Equal Opportunities statement in 1990, which noted that 'Women, Black people, Lesbians, Gay men, people with a disability, those of all social backgrounds, and, irrespective of marital status, age, religion, national origin and HIV status' would face no discrimination at the Union.[112] Such actions did not completely fend off hostility to minority groups, such as when the LGB office door was vandalised with offensive messages in 1993.[113] Other Union causes, like the boycott of Nestlé products across all cafés and bars on the grounds of its unethical marketing of formula milk for babies in developing countries, provoked mixed reactions from the student body. One student wrote in Pi that this decision marked 'the final descent of Union policy into the glorious abyss of political correctness', whilst others defended it as a moral action to take.[114]

Many of the tensions of this period were underpinned by the politics of the 1980s and early 1990s, which were fractious times for student unions across the UK. The governments of that period attempted to reduce their funding and redefine their status. UCL's Union argued in 1987 that 'Student Unions are facing the most concerted attack ever made by a government against their very existence'.[115] Sabbatical officers asked students to think of the philosophical arguments for education for its own sake and the importance of it being free. In response to the perceived undermining of Unions, some Sabbs wrote to students to say: 'we are not asking you to become a 'radical' but to question the wisdom of a country that does not invest adequately in its own future. Ask yourself whether education is a right or a privilege. Look objectively at the arguments against Student Unions and ultimately support the Student Union that is there to support you'.[116]

Offices for student newspaper *Pi* in the 1980s. Students' Union UCL.

Bar inside the Windeyer Building, 1990s.

The Union's Centenary and After

In 1993, the Union's official centenary year, hope was expressed that a brand-new building was finally on the horizon. It was not.[117] Instead, the Union had to make do by expanding via other smaller sites and buildings, like the Windeyer. One sabbatical officer in 1989–1990, Jon Leslie-Smith, who later became an architect, was able to use his skills to help re-design the space to at least make what was there more efficient to work in.[118] By the millennium, the Union was operating over six locations, offering services to 16,000 members.[119] It is worth remembering that one student had spoken for many at the time when, in 1960, he had said that 3,000 students at UCL was 'much too large a number'.[120]

Students in 'The Garage' before it was demolished in 1990. Students' Union UCL.

At 25 Gordon Street, the 2econd Floor Bar and Easy J's, sold a nutritious range of food, including fry ups, 'juicy burgers', fried chicken, chips, onion rings, pizza and ice cream. This space then doubled up into a club venue, with 'a state of the art, dangerously loud sound and light system'. On the other end of the second floor was Sandwich Street.[121] On the floor above, the Phineas Bar offered pub food.[122] Students wrote to *Pi* to complain that these venues were so cramped it was often necessary to think about bringing a gasmask because of the number of people smoking in such small rooms.[123] Capacity problems were made even more prominent when, in 2005, the number of people allowed into 25 Gordon Street was halved to 350, due to changed health and safety rules, seriously impacting Union finances. Around this time there was regular discussion in the student press about the Union being in 'crisis', with capacity cuts and student apathy preventing it from being as strong a force as it might otherwise be.[124] Even sabbatical officer elections did not generate a huge amount of interest. On one controversial occasion, it was alleged that students had been offered free entry to the popular cocktail night if they first voted in the annual sabbatical officer election. Perhaps unsurprisingly, that year's winner for each post was the candidate whose names was at the top of the list for each role![125] The *Cheese Grater* was launched as an alternative, satirical student publication in 2004.

How to better engage students was approached from different angles. In 2002, the Union's Student Volunteering Service was established, staffed by John Braime and Petra Wahlqvist (Braime continued to run the unit for the next twenty years). It was pitched as an exciting new service 'dedicated to helping students get involved with community action projects across London ... You can give as much or as little time as you like'. Students were encouraged to engage with one-off projects, like helping decorate a community centre, or longer-term placements. Union officer Frank Penter heralded the Volunteering Service as the first dedicated team focusing on volunteering opportunities for students in the UK.[126] The idea for a Volunteering Service had been raised by Sarah Douglas, who was widely considered a brilliant member of the Union staff. From 1988 to 2006, Sarah worked as Advice Manager and then as Membership Services Manager, before moving to the General Manager role at the Institute of Education's Students' Union. After her premature death, Sarah's family set up a Hardship Fund in her name, which still exists today, and which helps students at UCL overcome financial difficulties.[127]

UCL students and the Union played a role in supporting the community when terrorists blew themselves up on the London Underground and on a bus in 2005, with some of the bombs exploding close to UCL. As the Editor of *Pi* wrote in the aftermath of the tragedy, 'a wound has been left on the area around UCL ... we remember the images of blood-stained walls at Tavistock Square...'[128] This period also witnessed the beginnings of a change of tone in the way the Union communicated with students. There had long been a discrepancy between promoting club nights, heavily fuelled by cheap drinks and cut-price cocktails, versus wanting to promote responsible behaviour. In some cases, club nights were advertised with posters that, in hindsight, appear to be in extraordinarily bad taste. A review at the end of the 2000s, for example, changed the way women were presented in the advertisements for club nights, to make posters appear less sexist. At the same time, dedicated Union networks were established for black and minority ethnic students; disabled students; international students; LGBT+ students; students of faith and women students. This was done with the purpose of providing 'a forum for students to work together to raise awareness'.[129] The student population was becoming increasingly diverse, with many students not drinking alcohol, and this had a bearing on the change in focus and tone.

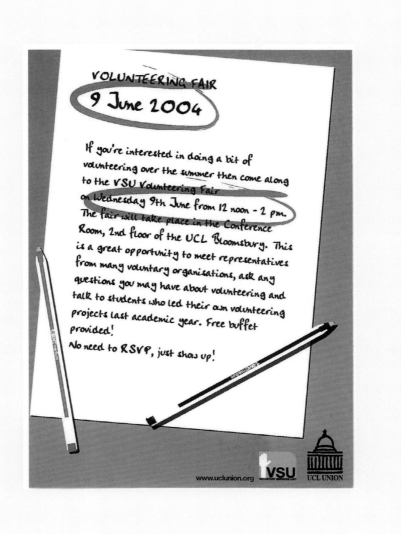

Poster for one of the first student volunteering fairs. UCL Special Collections.

A Rugby match between TeamUCL and King's, Varsity 2013. Students' Union UCL.

Freshers' Ball advert from the early 2000s. Students' Union UCL.

From the late 1990s onwards, the issue of tuition fees rose to the top of the agenda for the Union and the student body more broadly. There were high hopes for the Labour government that took office in 1997, after a long period of Conservative administrations which many had considered hostile to higher education. However, the new government introduced tuition fees in 1998. The following year, 160 UCL students withheld their fees as an act of protest.[130] Demonstrations were organised, with sabbatical officers writing to the student press in 2000 to encourage as many people as possible to join a march, with the rallying cry of 'get off your arses and DO SOMETHING NOW!'. Many UCL students also participated in the enormous national protests against the invasion of Iraq in 2003 and took part in local teach-ins and demonstrations.[131] So-called 'top-up' fees, introduced in 2004, were again met with anger by students.

UCL Stop the War Coalition poster, October 2003. Daniel Rogger collection.

Change and Challenge

A sense of discontentment continued. The 'austerity agenda' of the new Conservative-Liberal Democrat coalition government from 2010 and its plans to treble tuition fees to £9,000 per year for most UK students, was reported to have created an 'unprecedented political consciousness among the student body' and the 'biggest student movement since the 1970s'.[132] This rebellious mood spilled over into other issues, with students leading the resistance to the Carpenters Estate being developed by UCL as a new campus in Stratford, east London, which would have moved 700 people out of their homes. The Union saw itself as having 'won the day' when in May 2013 UCL pulled out of negotiations to purchase that land.[133]

UCL students celebrate London hosting the Olympic Games in 2012. Students Union UCL.

This spirit also funnelled into quite radical change in terms of the make-up of the Sabbatical officer team. In the early 2000s, the 'Sabb' officer roles were: Services and Events; Media and Communications; Education and Welfare; Clubs, Societies and Student Development; Finance and Administration; and Medical Students and Sites (for specific queries for medical, postgraduate or SSEES students).[134] There were some concerns about these jobs – Education and Welfare was a disproportionately large brief, for example – and the roles were restructured over time. In 2008 the Education and Welfare role was split in two, with a rejigged Communications and Services post included as part of the team.[135]

The biggest change in this regard came in the 2012–13 academic year, where the core team of six was expanded to ten. Whilst many of the roles were restructured or broken up, the headline-grabbing changes included a dedicated, full-time Women's Officer, and a BME (Black and Minority Ethnic) Students' Officer – the first of its kind in the UK.[136] Consequently, at the 2013 NUS Black Students' Conference, UCL was awarded 'Students' Union of the Year', where it was commended for setting a positive precedent. There were misgivings, however, with some expressing discomfort at pigeon-holing Black students in this way, and others arguing that a team of ten sabbaticals was simply too unwieldy. Whilst the pioneering nature of these roles were acknowledged, the team was later scaled back to six core officers to make the running of the Union more manageable. There were changes too within the student body. The merger of the Institute of Education with UCL in 2014 made UCL a majority postgraduate institution and brought with it the challenges of integrating a previously separate students' union.

Bar in the Institute of Education before it was refurbished in 2018. Students' Union UCL.

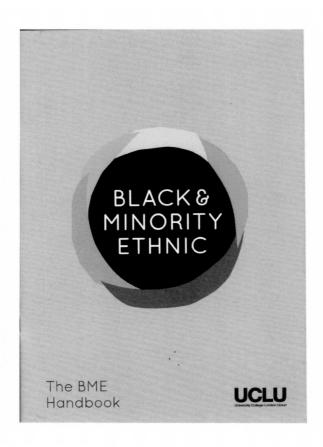

BME Handbook, 2013. Students' Union UCL.

Managing and running the Union continued to pose exciting challenges. For example, by 2014, the Union oversaw the administration of a huge 230 clubs and societies. Just a few of the more recently-established included: Capoeira Society, Cheerleading, Laser tag, Parkour, Ultimate Frisbee, Anime, Azerbaijan, Masaryk, Dinosaur Appreciation and Harry Potter Society.

It was not simply the growing size of the student body, or the number of sabbatical officers, that caused problems for the Union in the late 2000s and into the 2010s. For many, this period witnessed significant challenges of leadership made worse by inadequate offices and facilities. A difficult financial position with deficit budgets, under-investment, and cuts to services compounded by a challenging relationship with UCL, and falling levels of student engagement, relegated the Union to the peripheries of student life.

Appeal for candidates to stand for election, 2012. Students' Union UCL.

A Malaysian Society production in Bloomsbury Theatre, 2012.

Back at the Centre of Student Life

In 2015, changes began with the arrival of Ian Dancy as the Chief Executive of the Union – the new title was in line changes in students' unions across the country.[137] Over the course of three years, Dancy began a re-structuring and re-branding exercise to lay the foundations for the Union's future development. Other changes related to the political climate were taking place. In 2018, Students' Union sabbatical officers were involved in the campaign for UCL to acknowledge its historic role in legitimising Eugenics, leading to the establishment of the Eugenics Inquiry that reported in 2020.[138] It was this context that the next Chief Executive, John Dubber, inherited in 2019. He continued to instigate a more professional culture in the Union and make changes to improve support for the Sabbatical Officers and drive improved services for students. John remembers how:

> Working closely with the Sabbatical officer teams, we set out to set a much stronger future ambition for the Union to once again be one of the best in the country; to empower and support the Sabbs to be more successful influencers and leaders of the Union and ambassadors for students; to build a more effective relationship with UCL to deliver a great student experience; and to modernise and improve the Union's services.[139]

Over the next few years, these new staff and officer teams made progress and student engagement increased markedly while Union influence in UCL decision making also increased. The Union's democratic structures were refreshed based on a blueprint developed by Mahmud Rahman (Democracy, Operations and Community Officer, 2018–19) who created Policy Zones in place of the old Union Council. Gradually, the Union's finances were restored to health with a return to surplus budgets, enabling investment in new facilities. The Union started to attract more grant funding from UCL and its growing commercial income enabled the recruitment of more staff and expansion of services. New programmes such as Project Active and TeamUCL sports leagues enabled more students to participate in Union activity and also lead to record postgraduate participation levels.

Students' Union 5K Run, part of Project Active, first launched in 2022. Students' Union UCL.

Phineas bar in 2023. Students' Union UCL.

In a symbolic break with the past, Phineas was removed as the Union mascot in 2019. The Union bar in 25 Gordon Street had been named Phineas after the Union's 1993 centenary celebrations and the mascot was housed there. However, in 2019, the statue's initial links with a pro-Boer War demonstration in 1900 led to a debate about its future, and the Union Executive voted to remove Phineas from the bar and to dispense with it as the official mascot.

However, discussions about what to do with the former mascot, along with so much else, were put on hold when the Union was plunged into a crisis alongside the whole world. In March 2020, the UK government ordered the public to work from home to try to delay the spread of a novel coronavirus, Covid 19. The fundamentals of the Students' Union had, until this point, been about large groups of people meeting together in person for various purposes. Within a few days, the Union had closed all of its face-to-face services, moving to online support for students. The pandemic struck during the Union's election period, meaning campaigns had to move online. For some of the Sabbatical officers at the Union, March 2020 and subsequent months represented a steep learning curve. Ayman Benmati, (Sabbatical Officer 2020–22) was charged with representing the student voice at various high level and high-pressured UCL steering groups, where decisions that normally took weeks to make were being fast-tracked in days or even hours. He remembers how:

When we first got started it was really in the midst of the pandemic ... and then I got thrown into UCL meetings and they were in crisis management mode at that time ... loads of working groups and emergency meetings and it was very high energy, touch and go ... I got thrown into the middle of all that chaos on my first week and there'd be Vice Provosts of Education, experts in their fields: "so Ayman what do you think about this, we need to make a decision today". And it was completely overwhelming.[140]

Ayman Benmati, Education Officer, 2020–2022. Students' Union UCL.

For the student body, the pandemic offered opportunities but also posed grave challenges. Some found local volunteering opportunities, whilst others worked closely with academic departments to aid the transition to online learning. Hundreds of medical students worked as paid or volunteer healthcare support workers in response to the NHS's call to action. However, others naturally experienced challenges with their mental health, and suffered feelings of loneliness and anxiety having been separated from their friends.

The Union prioritised supporting students by building online communities. Many of its staff worked through the pandemic and unlike many other Unions it made no redundancies. The pandemic also saw the closure of the Student Central building on Malet Street, just outside the gates of UCL, that had for decades been home to the University of London Union, and was heavily used by UCL students. The Union worked with the local community to campaign against its closure including attempting to get the building listed. Since the easing of lockdowns, it was widely agreed that a concerted effort to return to a sense of pre-Covid 'normality' was successful.

Since the pandemic, the Union has continued a period of extensive renewal and development, with growing student engagement and satisfaction. It has set an aim to to one of the best student organsations in the world. In 2023, the Union worked with UCL to develop UCL's new Student Life Strategy which lays out a vision for a major expansion of extracurricular activity, a fitting way for the Union to pass its 130th anniversary milestone.

Students with masks on campus, 2021. Students' Union UCL.

Conclusion

For many students, 'the Union contains the essence of College life.'[141] It has certainly played a central role in the lives of hundreds of thousands of UCL students since 1893, but it is also important to acknowledge that every generation has contained students who are unaware of Union affairs and the role the it plays. Even former Sabbatical officers have conceded that the Union can sometimes feel like 'an enigma wrapped in mystery'.[142] In 1919, one student wrote that 'There are still too many ... at the college who are not of it ... They give nothing and as a consequence receive nothing'.[143] In 1959, on the eve of the Union's move into 25 Gordon Street, student officers wrote that 'all hopes for curing (apathy) ... are pinned on the new premises'.[144] To some extent, disengagement is a fact of student social and political life, despite the fact that, because of the 1994 Education Act, all students automatically become members of a students' union when they come to university. Whilst Sabbatical officers over the years have acknowledged this, they have also worked hard to increase the profile of the Union and to encourage more students to get involved. Some generations have succeeded in this more than others, but as the Union passes its 130th milestone, its engagement levels are now higher than ever.

The Union's development is due to many, especially the countless generations of sabbatical officers and staff of the Union. Current and future officers and staff will undoubtedly be able to say they are standing on the shoulders of giants. After their time as Union Officers and those involved in its wider activities, many went on to success in other ways too. Stafford Cripps, Chancellor of the Exchequer in a pivotal period for Britain from 1947–1950, was Union President in 1910. Two current members of the House of Lords, Tom McNally and John Shipley, are former Presidents. Notable people like the journalist Bel Mooney and film director Christopher Nolan participated in the Union's activities during their time as students.

Current officers are now overseeing an organisation that has hugely improved its services in the past few years and is now in very good health. However, with more than 50,000 students at UCL in the 2020s, the challenges the Union faces in trying to represent these are not inconsiderable. The largest postgraduate and international student communities in the UK, a new UCL site at Stratford in East London, as well as the continued growth of the main Bloomsbury campus will continue to provide unrivalled opportunities for the Union the future, as well as significant challenges.

The 2023–24 Sabbatical Officers. Students' Union UCL.
From top left: Aria Xingni Shi, Activities & Engagement Officer. Shaban Chaudhary, Education Officer.
Ahmad Ismail, Equity & Inclusion Officer. Issy Smith, Postgraduate Officer. Mary McHarg, Union Affairs Officer.

A live performance of the Salsa Society at the Union's 2023 Welcome Fair. Students' Union UCL.

As the Union celebrates its 130th birthday, a sense of pride in the ground-breaking new Student Life Strategy agreed with UCL, is clear. This will markedly increase extra-curricular activities, seeking as it does to encourage more students to engage with sport and arts programmes; promote volunteering opportunities and inter-cultural engagement; as well as support greater engagement with students and their departmental societies. Key to the future will clearly be a bigger and better home for the Union that is able to meet the needs of students today and in the future. A main building branded temporary and inadequate in the mid-1950s still acts as the hub of the Union today. Better facilities remain the number one priority for this generation of student leaders, as Students' Union UCL prepares to play an even more central role in the life of UCL in the coming years.

Students' at UCL East campus, opened in 2022. Students' Union UCL.

Notes

1 UCL Film Soc newsreel 44, 1971.

2 UCL Annual Report, 1957–58, 18. UCL Special Collections.

3 David Taylor, *The Godless Students of Gower Street* (London: University College London, 1968), 11–12.

4 Negley Harte, John North and Georgina Brewis, *The World of UCL* (London: UCL Press, 2018), 13.

5 Harte, North and Brewis, *World of UCL*, 73.

6 James Bates and Carol Ibbetson, *The World of UCL Union: 1893–1993* (London: UCL Union, 1994), 76.

7 Harte, North and Brewis, *World of UCL*, 90.

8 Students' Union Handbook, 1915–16. UCL Special Collections.

9 Harte, North and Brewis, *World of UCL*, 89.

10 Harte, North and Brewis, *World of UCL*, 134.

11 Bates and Ibbetson, *UCL Union,* 88.

12 Bates and Ibbetson, *UCL Union*, 88.

13 Taylor, *Godless Students*, 22.

14 Harte, North and Brewis, *World of UCL*, 90.

15 Bates and Ibbetson, *UCL Union*, 6.

16 Harte, North and Brewis, *World of UCL*, 90.

17 Harte, North and Brewis, *World of UCL*, 90.

18 Bates and Ibbetson, *UCL Union*, 28

19 Bates and Ibbetson, *UCL Union*, 13–14.

20 Harte, North and Brewis, *World of UCL*, 140.

21 Bates and Ibbetson, *UCL Union*, 101.

22 Bates and Ibbetson, *UCL Union*, 100.

23 Students' Union Handbook, 1915–16, 80.

24 Bates and Ibbetson, *UCL Union*, 88–89.

25 Harte, North and Brewis, *World of UCL*, 149.

26 Georgina Brewis, *A Social History of Student Volunteering: Britain and Beyond, 1880-1980* (New York: Palgrave Macmillan, 2014), 181; Carol Dyhouse, *Students: A Gendered History* (London: Routledge, 2005).

27 Harte, North and Brewis, *World of UCL*, 153-57.

28 Students' Union Handbook, 1915–16.

29 Students' Union Handbook, 1919–20, 12

30 Harte, North and Brewis, *World of UCL*, 157, 172.

31 Georgina Brewis, Sarah Hellawell and Daniel Laqua, 'Rebuilding the Universities after the Great War: Ex-Service Students, Scholarships and the Reconstruction of Student Life in England', *History* vol. 105 (2020): 82–106.

32 Bates and Ibbetson, *UCL Union*, 14.

33 Harte, North and Brewis, *World of UCL*, 171.

34 Students' Union Handbook, 1929–30.

35 Students' Union Handbook, 1934–35; See also UCL Calendars.

36 Students' Union Handbook, 1927–28, 154–55.

37 Students' Union Handbook, 1921–22.

38 Bates and Ibbetson, *UCL Union*, 29.

39 *The UCL Student's Songbook* (London: University of London, University College, 1926).

40 Bates and Ibbetson, *UCL Union*, 81, 101.

41 Harte, North and Brewis, *World of UCL*, 201–202.

42 Harte, North and Brewis, *World of UCL*, 202.

43 Students' Union Handbook, 1941–42, preface.

44 Generation UCL interview with Diana Armfield, conducted by Sam Blaxland, 24 May 2022.

45 Students' Union Handbook, 1946–47.

46 Bates and Ibbetson, *UCL Union*, 29.

47 Students' Union Handbook, 1946–47.

48 Generation UCL interview with Professor Alwyn Davies, conducted by Sam Blaxland, 10 January 2023.

49 Bates and Ibbetson, *UCL Union*, 19.

50 Harte, North and Brewis, *World of UCL*, 235; Bates and Ibbetson, *UCL Union*, 91–96.

51 Harte, North and Brewis, *World of UCL*, 217.

52 UCL Annual Report 1948–49, 87.

53 Bates and Ibbetson, *UCL Union*, 82.

54 Students' Union Handbook, 1947–48, 30.

55 UCL Annual Report, 1951–52, 17.

56 Students' Union Handbook, 1947–48, 9.

57 Bates and Ibbetson, UCL Union, 130.

58 Students' Union Handbook, 1950–51, 61.

59 Bates and Ibbetson, *UCL Union*, 29.

60 UCL Annual Report, 1948–1949, 86. The Debating Society was given a chamber in the main building in 1953.

61 UCL Annual Report, 1949–1950, 77.

62 UCL Annual Report, 1949–1950, 77; UCL Annual Report, 1954–55, 16; Generation UCL interview with Stuart Richman, conducted by Sam Blaxland, 26 May 2022.

63 UCL Film Soc newsreel 21, c.1960.

64 Harte, North and Brewis, *World of UCL*, 217.

65 UCL Annual Report, 1954–55, 15.

66 UCL Annual Report, 1958–59.

67 Bates and Ibbetson, *UCL Union*, 62; Generation UCL interview with Rosalind Levacic, conducted by Sam Blaxland, 15 June 2022.

68 *Velesh*, 1970s. UCL Special Collections.

69 UCL Annual Report, 1956–57, 8.

70 Students' Union handbook, 1955–56.

71 UCL Annual Report, 1957–58, Appendix VIII.

72 Bates and Ibbetson, *UCL Union*, 21.

73 Bates and Ibbetson, *UCL Union*, 82.

74 Bates and Ibbetson, *UCL Union*, 84.

75 See various Students' Union Handbooks.

76 Generation UCL interview with Dr Toni Griffiths, conducted by Sam Blaxland, 8 March 2023.

77 UCL Film Soc newsreel 26, 1962.

78 UCL Film Soc newsreel 20, 1959.

79 Bates and Ibbetson, *UCL Union*, 119.

80 Bates and Ibbetson, *UCL Union*, 120; Generation UCL interview with Lord McNally, conducted by Sam Blaxland, 23 May 2022.

81 Students' Union Handbook, 1961–62.

82 Students' Union handbook, 1968–69, 84.

83 Students' Union handbook, 1966–67, 5.

84 Harte, North and Brewis, *World of UCL*, 232.

85 Bates and Ibbetson, *UCL Union*, 131.

86 UCL Annual Report 1968–69, 8.

87 Bates and Ibbetson, *UCL Union*, 96.

88 Harte, North and Brewis, *World of UCL*, 267.

89 Bates and Ibbetson, *UCL Union*, 96.

90 For a wider discussion, see Bates and Ibbetson, *UCL Union*, chapter 3.

91 Generation UCL interview with Jamie Gardiner, conducted by Sam Blaxland, 1 September 2022.

92 Students' Union Handbook, 1972–73, 44.

93 Bates and Ibbetson, *UCL Union*, 63

94 David Malcolm, 'A Curious Courage: The Origin of Gay Rights Campaigning in the National Union of Students', *History of Education*, 47, 1 (2018): 73–86; Bates and Ibbetson, *UCL Union*, 107.

95 Students' Union Handbook, 1975–76, 47.

96 Students' Union Handbook, 1973–74, 55.

97 Harte, North and Brewis, *World of UCL*, 285–6; Bates and Ibbetson, *UCL Union*, 23.

98 Bates and Ibbetson, *UCL Union*, 107.

99 Students' Union Handbook, 1976–77, 45.

100 Harte, North and Brewis, *World of UCL*, 258.

101 Students' Union Handbook, 1978–79, 19.

102 Bates and Ibbetson, *UCL Union*, 132.

103 Students' Union Handbook, 1984–85.

104 Bates and Ibbetson, *UCL Union*, 132-33

105 Bates and Ibbetson, *UCL Union*, 133.

106 Generation UCL interview with Spencer Gore, conducted by Sam Blaxland, 4 March 2023.

107 Harte, North and Brewis, *World of UCL*, 284.

108 Bates and Ibbetson, *UCL Union*, 94

109 Students' Union Handbook, 1986–87.

110 Students' Union Handbook, 1991–92, 53.

111 Students' Union Handbook, 1989–90.

112 Students' Union Handbook, 1991–92, 5.

113 *Pi*, 31 January 1994, 7.
114 *Pi*, January 1995.
115 Students' Union Handbook, 1987–88.
116 Students' Union Handbook, 1987–88.
117 Bates and Ibbetson, *UCL Union*, 39.
118 Generation UCL interview with Jon Leslie-Smith, conducted by Sam Blaxland, 17 May 2023
119 Students' Union Handbook, 1999–2000.
120 UCL Film Soc newsreel 23, 1960.
121 Students' Union Handbook, 1997–98.
122 Students' Union Handbook, 1997–98.
123 *Pi*, November 1993.
124 See, for example, 'UCL: a Union in Crisis?', *Pi*, Issue 654, 4.
125 *Pi*, 3 April 1995.
126 *Pi*, Issue 632.
127 Generation UCL interview with Katerina Alexandropoulou, conducted by Sam Blaxland, 11 May 2023.
128 *Pi*, Issue 652.
129 Students' Union Handbook, 2008–09, 20.
130 *Pi*, Issue 607.
131 *Pi*, Issue 637; Iraq War Scrapbooks compiled by Daniel Rogger, UCL Special Collections.
132 Students' Union UCL Impact Report, 2011–12, 3.
133 Students' Union UCL Impact Report, 2012–13, 5.
134 Students' Union Handbook, 2004.
135 Students' Union Handbook, 2008–09.
136 Students' Union UCL Impact Report, 2012–13; Students' Union Handbook, 2013–14.
137 https://www.thirdsector.co.uk/student-unions-keen-register-commission/governance/article/644776
138 'Inheriting Galton: The people working to make UCL less racist', *The Cheese Grater*, March 2018.
139 Information supplied by John Dubber to Sam Blaxland, 2023.
140 Generation UCL interview with Ayman Benmati, conducted by Sam Blaxand, 7 July 2022.
141 Michael Freeman, 'Foreword', Bates and Ibbetson, *UCL Union*.
142 Students' Union Handbook, 1976–77, 2.
143 Bates and Ibbetson, *UCL Union*, 89.
144 Students' Union Handbook, 1958–59.

Further Reading

Robert Anderson, *British Universities: Past and Present* (London: Hambledon Continuum, 2006).

James Bates and Carol Ibbetson, *The World of UCL Union, 1893–1993* (London: UCL Union, 1994).

Hugh Hale Bellot, *University College London, 1826–1926* (London: University of London Press, 1929).

Georgina Brewis, *A Social History of Student Volunteering: Britain and Beyond, 1880-1980* (New York: Palgrave Macmillan, 2014).

Georgina Brewis, Sarah Hellawell and Daniel Laqua, 'Rebuilding the Universities after the Great War: Ex-Service Students, Scholarships and the Reconstruction of Student Life in England', *History*, vol. 105 (2020): 82–106.

Carol Dyhouse, *Students: A Gendered History* (London: Routledge, 2005).

Negley Harte, John North and Georgina Brewis, *The World of UCL* (UCL Press, 2018).

Caroline Hoefferle, *British Student Activism in the Long Sixties* (London: Routledge, 2013).

David Malcolm, 'A Curious Courage: The Origin of Gay Rights Campaigning in the National Union of Students', *History of Education* 47, 1 (2018): 73–86.

Sheldon Rothblatt, 'London: A Metropolitan University?', in Bender (ed.), *The University and the City: From Medieval Origins to the Present* (Oxford: Oxford University Press, 1988).

David Taylor, The Godless Students of Gower Street (London: University College London Union, 1968).

UCL Special Collections

We are grateful to UCL Special Collections for allowing us to reproduce many of the images in this publication.

UCL Records within UCL Special Collections look after UCL's institutional archive, books and other material connected with UCL's History. UCL's Calendars, student magazines and other sources are digitised and available to read online. Find out more: https://www.ucl.ac.uk/library/special-collections

Students working in the library in the late 19th-century. UCL Special Collections.